This BUCKET LIST
was created by:

_____

and

_____

Bucket List Table of Contents

01	
02	
03	
04	
05	
06	
07	
08	
09	
10	
11	
12	
13	
14	
15	
16	
17	
18	
19	
20	

Bucket List Table of Contents

21	
22	
23	
24	
25	
26	
27	
28	
29	
30	
31	
32	
33	
34	
35	
36	
37	
38	
39	
40	

Bucket List Table of Contents

41	
42	
43	
44	
45	
46	
47	
48	
49	
50	
51	
52	
53	
54	
55	
56	
57	
58	
59	
60	

Bucket List Table of Contents

Bucket List Table of Contents

81	
82	
83	
84	
85	
86	
87	
88	
89	
90	
91	
92	
93	
94	
95	
96	
97	
98	
99	
100	

01 _____
_____
_____

WHY DO WE WANT TO DO THIS? _____
_____
_____

WHAT DO WE NEED TO DO TO PREPARE?
_____
_____

💜 WE DID IT! 💜

DATE: _____ LOCATION: _____

WHAT HAPPENED? _____
_____
_____
_____
_____

WHAT WE LOVED: _____
_____
_____
_____

WHAT WE LEARNED:_____
_____
_____

💜

02
_____
_____
_____

WHY DO WE WANT TO DO THIS? _____
_____
_____

WHAT DO WE NEED TO DO TO PREPARE?
_____
_____

♥ WE DID IT! ♥

DATE: _____ LOCATION: _____

WHAT HAPPENED? _____
_____
_____
_____
_____

WHAT WE LOVED: _____
_____
_____
_____

WHAT WE LEARNED: _____
_____
_____

♥

03

_____

_____

_____

WHY DO WE WANT TO DO THIS? _____

_____

_____

WHAT DO WE NEED TO DO TO PREPARE?

_____

_____

♥ WE DID IT! ♥

DATE: _____   LOCATION: _____

WHAT HAPPENED? _____

_____

_____

_____

_____

WHAT WE LOVED: _____

_____

_____

_____

WHAT WE LEARNED:_____

_____

_____

♥

04 _____
_____
_____

WHY DO WE WANT TO DO THIS? _____
_____
_____

WHAT DO WE NEED TO DO TO PREPARE?
_____
_____

♥ WE DID IT! ♥

DATE: _____ LOCATION: _____

WHAT HAPPENED? _____
_____
_____
_____
_____

WHAT WE LOVED: _____
_____
_____
_____

WHAT WE LEARNED: _____
_____
_____

♥

05 _____
_____
_____

WHY DO WE WANT TO DO THIS? _____
_____
_____

WHAT DO WE NEED TO DO TO PREPARE?
_____
_____

♥ WE DID IT! ♥

DATE: _____ LOCATION: _____
WHAT HAPPENED? _____
_____
_____
_____
_____

WHAT WE LOVED: _____
_____
_____
_____

WHAT WE LEARNED:_____
_____
_____

♥

06 _____
_____
_____

WHY DO WE WANT TO DO THIS? _____
_____
_____

WHAT DO WE NEED TO DO TO PREPARE?
_____
_____

♥ WE DID IT! ♥

DATE: _____ LOCATION: _____

WHAT HAPPENED? _____
_____
_____
_____
_____

WHAT WE LOVED: _____
_____
_____
_____

WHAT WE LEARNED:_____
_____
_____

♥

07

_____
_____
_____

WHY DO WE WANT TO DO THIS? _____
_____
_____

WHAT DO WE NEED TO DO TO PREPARE?
_____
_____

♥ WE DID IT! ♥

DATE: _____   LOCATION: _____

WHAT HAPPENED? _____
_____
_____
_____
_____

WHAT WE LOVED: _____
_____
_____
_____

WHAT WE LEARNED: _____
_____
_____

♥

08 _____
_____
_____

WHY DO WE WANT TO DO THIS? _____
_____
_____

WHAT DO WE NEED TO DO TO PREPARE?
_____
_____

♥ WE DID IT! ♥

DATE: _____ LOCATION: _____

WHAT HAPPENED? _____
_____
_____
_____
_____

WHAT WE LOVED: _____
_____
_____
_____

WHAT WE LEARNED:_____
_____
_____

♥

09 _____
_____
_____
_____

WHY DO WE WANT TO DO THIS? _____
_____
_____

WHAT DO WE NEED TO DO TO PREPARE?
_____
_____

♥ WE DID IT! ♥

DATE: _____ LOCATION: _____

WHAT HAPPENED? _____
_____
_____
_____
_____

WHAT WE LOVED: _____
_____
_____
_____

WHAT WE LEARNED:_____
_____
_____

♥

10

_____
_____
_____

WHY DO WE WANT TO DO THIS? _____
_____
_____

WHAT DO WE NEED TO DO TO PREPARE?
_____
_____

♥ WE DID IT! ♥

DATE: _____ LOCATION: _____

WHAT HAPPENED? _____
_____
_____
_____
_____

WHAT WE LOVED: _____
_____
_____
_____

WHAT WE LEARNED:_____
_____
_____

♥

11

WHY DO WE WANT TO DO THIS? _____

_____

_____

WHAT DO WE NEED TO DO TO PREPARE?

_____

_____

 WE DID IT!

DATE: _____ LOCATION: _____

WHAT HAPPENED? _____

_____

_____

_____

_____

WHAT WE LOVED: _____

_____

_____

_____

WHAT WE LEARNED:_____

_____

_____

12 _____
_____
_____

WHY DO WE WANT TO DO THIS? _____

_____

_____

WHAT DO WE NEED TO DO TO PREPARE?

_____

_____

♥ WE DID IT! ♥

DATE: _____ LOCATION: _____

WHAT HAPPENED? _____

_____

_____

_____

_____

WHAT WE LOVED: _____

_____

_____

WHAT WE LEARNED: _____

_____

_____

♥

13

_____
_____
_____

WHY DO WE WANT TO DO THIS? _____
_____
_____

WHAT DO WE NEED TO DO TO PREPARE?
_____
_____

♥ WE DID IT! ♥

DATE: _____ LOCATION: _____

WHAT HAPPENED? _____
_____
_____
_____
_____

WHAT WE LOVED: _____
_____
_____
_____

WHAT WE LEARNED: _____
_____
_____

♥

14

_____
_____
_____

WHY DO WE WANT TO DO THIS? _____
_____
_____

WHAT DO WE NEED TO DO TO PREPARE?
_____
_____

 WE DID IT! ♥

DATE: _____ LOCATION: _____

WHAT HAPPENED? _____
_____
_____
_____
_____

WHAT WE LOVED: _____
_____
_____
_____

WHAT WE LEARNED:_____
_____
_____

♥

15

_____
_____
_____

WHY DO WE WANT TO DO THIS? _____
_____
_____

WHAT DO WE NEED TO DO TO PREPARE?
_____
_____

 WE DID IT! ♥

DATE: _____ LOCATION: _____

WHAT HAPPENED? _____
_____
_____
_____
_____

WHAT WE LOVED: _____
_____
_____
_____

WHAT WE LEARNED: _____
_____
_____

♥

16

_____
_____
_____

WHY DO WE WANT TO DO THIS? _____
_____
_____

WHAT DO WE NEED TO DO TO PREPARE?
_____
_____

♥ WE DID IT! ♥

DATE: _____ LOCATION: _____

WHAT HAPPENED? _____
_____
_____
_____
_____

WHAT WE LOVED: _____
_____
_____
_____

WHAT WE LEARNED:_____
_____
_____

♥

17

_____
_____
_____

WHY DO WE WANT TO DO THIS? _____
_____
_____

WHAT DO WE NEED TO DO TO PREPARE?
_____
_____

♥ WE DID IT! ♥

DATE: _____ LOCATION: _____

WHAT HAPPENED? _____
_____
_____
_____
_____

WHAT WE LOVED: _____
_____
_____

WHAT WE LEARNED:_____
_____
_____

♥

18

_____
_____
_____

WHY DO WE WANT TO DO THIS? _____
_____
_____

WHAT DO WE NEED TO DO TO PREPARE?
_____
_____

♥ WE DID IT! ♥

DATE: _____ LOCATION: _____

WHAT HAPPENED? _____
_____
_____
_____
_____

WHAT WE LOVED: _____
_____
_____
_____

WHAT WE LEARNED: _____
_____
_____

♥

19

_____
_____
_____

WHY DO WE WANT TO DO THIS? _____
_____
_____

WHAT DO WE NEED TO DO TO PREPARE?
_____
_____

♥ WE DID IT! ♥

DATE: _____ LOCATION: _____

WHAT HAPPENED? _____
_____
_____
_____
_____

WHAT WE LOVED: _____
_____
_____
_____

WHAT WE LEARNED:_____
_____
_____

♥

20 _____
_____
_____

WHY DO WE WANT TO DO THIS? _____
_____
_____

WHAT DO WE NEED TO DO TO PREPARE?
_____
_____

 WE DID IT! ♥

DATE: _____   LOCATION: _____

WHAT HAPPENED? _____
_____
_____
_____
_____

WHAT WE LOVED: _____
_____
_____
_____

WHAT WE LEARNED: _____
_____
_____

♥

21

_____
_____
_____

WHY DO WE WANT TO DO THIS? _____
_____
_____

WHAT DO WE NEED TO DO TO PREPARE?
_____
_____

 WE DID IT! ♥

DATE: _____ LOCATION: _____

WHAT HAPPENED? _____
_____
_____
_____
_____

WHAT WE LOVED: _____
_____
_____
_____

WHAT WE LEARNED:_____
_____
_____

♥

22

_____
_____
_____

WHY DO WE WANT TO DO THIS? _____
_____
_____

WHAT DO WE NEED TO DO TO PREPARE?
_____
_____

♥ WE DID IT! ♥

DATE: _____ LOCATION: _____

WHAT HAPPENED? _____
_____
_____
_____
_____

WHAT WE LOVED: _____
_____
_____
_____

WHAT WE LEARNED:_____
_____
_____

♥

23

_____
_____
_____

WHY DO WE WANT TO DO THIS? _____
_____
_____

WHAT DO WE NEED TO DO TO PREPARE?
_____
_____

 WE DID IT! ♥

DATE: _____ LOCATION: _____

WHAT HAPPENED? _____
_____
_____
_____
_____

WHAT WE LOVED: _____
_____
_____
_____

WHAT WE LEARNED: _____
_____
_____

24 _____
_____
_____

WHY DO WE WANT TO DO THIS? _____
_____
_____

WHAT DO WE NEED TO DO TO PREPARE?
_____
_____

♥ WE DID IT! ♥

DATE: _____ LOCATION: _____

WHAT HAPPENED? _____
_____
_____
_____
_____

WHAT WE LOVED: _____
_____
_____
_____

WHAT WE LEARNED:_____
_____
_____

♥

25

_____
_____
_____

WHY DO WE WANT TO DO THIS? _____
_____
_____

WHAT DO WE NEED TO DO TO PREPARE?
_____
_____

 WE DID IT! ♥

DATE: _____ LOCATION: _____

WHAT HAPPENED? _____
_____
_____
_____
_____

WHAT WE LOVED: _____
_____
_____
_____

WHAT WE LEARNED:_____
_____
_____

♥

26

_____
_____
_____

WHY DO WE WANT TO DO THIS? _____
_____
_____

WHAT DO WE NEED TO DO TO PREPARE?
_____
_____

 WE DID IT! ♥

DATE: _____ LOCATION: _____

WHAT HAPPENED? _____
_____
_____
_____
_____

WHAT WE LOVED: _____
_____
_____
_____

WHAT WE LEARNED:_____
_____
_____

27 _____
_____
_____

WHY DO WE WANT TO DO THIS? _____
_____
_____

WHAT DO WE NEED TO DO TO PREPARE?
_____
_____

♥ **WE DID IT!** ♥

DATE: _____ LOCATION: _____
WHAT HAPPENED? _____
_____
_____
_____
_____

WHAT WE LOVED: _____
_____
_____
_____

WHAT WE LEARNED:_____
_____
_____

♥

28

_____
_____
_____

WHY DO WE WANT TO DO THIS? _____
_____
_____

WHAT DO WE NEED TO DO TO PREPARE?
_____
_____

♥ WE DID IT! ♥

DATE: _____ LOCATION: _____

WHAT HAPPENED? _____
_____
_____
_____
_____

WHAT WE LOVED: _____
_____
_____
_____

WHAT WE LEARNED: _____
_____
_____

♥

29

_____
_____
_____

WHY DO WE WANT TO DO THIS? _____
_____
_____

WHAT DO WE NEED TO DO TO PREPARE?
_____
_____

♥ WE DID IT! ♥

DATE: _____ LOCATION: _____

WHAT HAPPENED? _____
_____
_____
_____
_____

WHAT WE LOVED: _____
_____
_____

WHAT WE LEARNED:_____
_____
_____

♥

30

_____
_____
_____

WHY DO WE WANT TO DO THIS? _____
_____
_____

WHAT DO WE NEED TO DO TO PREPARE?
_____
_____

 WE DID IT! ♥

DATE: _____ LOCATION: _____

WHAT HAPPENED? _____
_____
_____
_____
_____

WHAT WE LOVED: _____
_____
_____
_____

WHAT WE LEARNED:_____
_____
_____

♥

31 _____
_____
_____

WHY DO WE WANT TO DO THIS? _____
_____
_____

WHAT DO WE NEED TO DO TO PREPARE?
_____
_____

♥ WE DID IT! ♥

DATE: _____ LOCATION: _____

WHAT HAPPENED? _____
_____
_____
_____
_____

WHAT WE LOVED: _____
_____
_____
_____

WHAT WE LEARNED:_____
_____
_____

♥

32

_____
_____
_____

WHY DO WE WANT TO DO THIS? _____
_____
_____

WHAT DO WE NEED TO DO TO PREPARE?
_____
_____

♥ WE DID IT! ♥

DATE: _____ LOCATION: _____

WHAT HAPPENED? _____
_____
_____
_____
_____

WHAT WE LOVED: _____
_____
_____
_____

WHAT WE LEARNED:_____
_____
_____

♥

33

_____
_____
_____

WHY DO WE WANT TO DO THIS? _____
_____
_____

WHAT DO WE NEED TO DO TO PREPARE?
_____
_____

 ♥ WE DID IT! ♥

DATE: _____   LOCATION: _____

WHAT HAPPENED? _____
_____
_____
_____
_____

WHAT WE LOVED: _____
_____
_____
_____

WHAT WE LEARNED: _____
_____
_____

♥

34

_____
_____
_____

WHY DO WE WANT TO DO THIS? _____
_____
_____

WHAT DO WE NEED TO DO TO PREPARE?
_____
_____

♥ WE DID IT! ♥

DATE: _____ LOCATION: _____

WHAT HAPPENED? _____
_____
_____
_____
_____

WHAT WE LOVED: _____
_____
_____
_____

WHAT WE LEARNED: _____
_____
_____

♥

35

_____
_____
_____

WHY DO WE WANT TO DO THIS? _____
_____
_____

WHAT DO WE NEED TO DO TO PREPARE?
_____
_____

♥ WE DID IT! ♥

DATE: _____ LOCATION: _____

WHAT HAPPENED? _____
_____
_____
_____
_____

WHAT WE LOVED: `_____
_____
_____
_____

WHAT WE LEARNED: _____
_____
_____

♥

36

_____
_____
_____

WHY DO WE WANT TO DO THIS? _____
_____
_____

WHAT DO WE NEED TO DO TO PREPARE?
_____
_____

♥ WE DID IT! ♥

DATE: _____ LOCATION: _____

WHAT HAPPENED? _____
_____
_____
_____
_____

WHAT WE LOVED: _____
_____
_____
_____

WHAT WE LEARNED: _____
_____
_____

♥

37

_____
_____
_____

WHY DO WE WANT TO DO THIS? _____
_____
_____

WHAT DO WE NEED TO DO TO PREPARE?
_____
_____

♥ WE DID IT! ♥

DATE: _____ LOCATION: _____

WHAT HAPPENED? _____
_____
_____
_____
_____

WHAT WE LOVED: _____
_____
_____
_____

WHAT WE LEARNED:_____
_____
_____

♥

38 _____
_____
_____

WHY DO WE WANT TO DO THIS? _____
_____
_____

WHAT DO WE NEED TO DO TO PREPARE?
_____
_____

♥ WE DID IT! ♥

DATE: _____ LOCATION: _____

WHAT HAPPENED? _____
_____
_____
_____
_____

WHAT WE LOVED: _____
_____
_____
_____

WHAT WE LEARNED: _____
_____
_____

39

_____
_____
_____

WHY DO WE WANT TO DO THIS? _____
_____
_____

WHAT DO WE NEED TO DO TO PREPARE?
_____
_____

♥ WE DID IT! ♥

DATE: _____ LOCATION: _____

WHAT HAPPENED? _____
_____
_____
_____
_____

WHAT WE LOVED: _____
_____
_____

WHAT WE LEARNED:_____
_____
_____

♥

40

_____
_____
_____

WHY DO WE WANT TO DO THIS? _____
_____
_____

WHAT DO WE NEED TO DO TO PREPARE?
_____
_____

 WE DID IT! ♥

DATE: _____ LOCATION: _____

WHAT HAPPENED? _____
_____
_____
_____
_____

WHAT WE LOVED: _____
_____
_____
_____

WHAT WE LEARNED: _____
_____
_____

♥

41

_____
_____
_____

WHY DO WE WANT TO DO THIS? _____
_____
_____

WHAT DO WE NEED TO DO TO PREPARE?
_____
_____

♥ WE DID IT! ♥

DATE: _____ LOCATION: _____

WHAT HAPPENED? _____
_____
_____
_____
_____

WHAT WE LOVED: _____
_____
_____

WHAT WE LEARNED:_____
_____
_____

♥

42

_____
_____
_____

WHY DO WE WANT TO DO THIS? _____
_____
_____

WHAT DO WE NEED TO DO TO PREPARE?
_____
_____

♥ WE DID IT! ♥

DATE: _____ LOCATION: _____

WHAT HAPPENED? _____
_____
_____
_____
_____

WHAT WE LOVED: _____
_____
_____
_____

WHAT WE LEARNED:_____
_____
_____

♥

43

_____
_____
_____

WHY DO WE WANT TO DO THIS? _____
_____
_____

WHAT DO WE NEED TO DO TO PREPARE?
_____
_____

♥ WE DID IT! ♥

DATE: _____ LOCATION: _____

WHAT HAPPENED? _____
_____
_____
_____
_____

WHAT WE LOVED: _____
_____
_____
_____

WHAT WE LEARNED:_____
_____
_____

♥

44 _____

_____

_____

WHY DO WE WANT TO DO THIS? _____

_____

_____

WHAT DO WE NEED TO DO TO PREPARE?

_____

_____

 WE DID IT! 💜

DATE: _____ LOCATION: _____

WHAT HAPPENED? _____

_____

_____

_____

_____

WHAT WE LOVED: _____

_____

_____

_____

WHAT WE LEARNED:_____

_____

_____

45

_____
_____
_____

WHY DO WE WANT TO DO THIS? _____
_____
_____

WHAT DO WE NEED TO DO TO PREPARE?
_____
_____

♥ WE DID IT! ♥

DATE: _____ LOCATION: _____

WHAT HAPPENED? _____
_____
_____
_____
_____

WHAT WE LOVED: _____
_____
_____
_____

WHAT WE LEARNED:_____
_____
_____

♥

46

_____
_____
_____

WHY DO WE WANT TO DO THIS? _____
_____
_____

WHAT DO WE NEED TO DO TO PREPARE?
_____
_____

♥ WE DID IT! ♥

DATE: _____ LOCATION: _____

WHAT HAPPENED? _____
_____
_____
_____
_____

WHAT WE LOVED: _____
_____
_____
_____

WHAT WE LEARNED:_____
_____
_____

♥

47 _____
_____
_____

WHY DO WE WANT TO DO THIS? _____
_____
_____

WHAT DO WE NEED TO DO TO PREPARE?
_____
_____

♥ WE DID IT! ♥

DATE: _____ LOCATION: _____
WHAT HAPPENED? _____
_____
_____
_____
_____

WHAT WE LOVED: _____
_____
_____
_____

WHAT WE LEARNED: _____
_____
_____

♥

48

_____
_____
_____

WHY DO WE WANT TO DO THIS? _____
_____
_____

WHAT DO WE NEED TO DO TO PREPARE?
_____
_____

 WE DID IT!

DATE: _____ LOCATION: _____

WHAT HAPPENED? _____
_____
_____
_____
_____

WHAT WE LOVED: _____
_____
_____
_____

WHAT WE LEARNED: _____
_____
_____

49

_____
_____
_____
_____

WHY DO WE WANT TO DO THIS? _____
_____
_____

WHAT DO WE NEED TO DO TO PREPARE?
_____
_____

♥ WE DID IT! ♥

DATE: _____ LOCATION: _____

WHAT HAPPENED? _____
_____
_____
_____
_____

WHAT WE LOVED: _____
_____
_____
_____

WHAT WE LEARNED:_____
_____
_____

♥

50 _____
_____
_____

WHY DO WE WANT TO DO THIS? _____
_____
_____

WHAT DO WE NEED TO DO TO PREPARE?
_____
_____

♥ WE DID IT! ♥

DATE: _____ LOCATION: _____

WHAT HAPPENED? _____
_____
_____
_____
_____

WHAT WE LOVED: _____
_____
_____
_____

WHAT WE LEARNED: _____
_____
_____

♥

51

_____
_____
_____

WHY DO WE WANT TO DO THIS? _____
_____
_____

WHAT DO WE NEED TO DO TO PREPARE?
_____
_____

♥ WE DID IT! ♥

DATE: _____ LOCATION: _____

WHAT HAPPENED? _____
_____
_____
_____
_____

WHAT WE LOVED: _____
_____
_____
_____

WHAT WE LEARNED:_____
_____
_____

♥

52

_____
_____
_____

WHY DO WE WANT TO DO THIS? _____
_____
_____

WHAT DO WE NEED TO DO TO PREPARE?
_____
_____

♥ WE DID IT! ♥

DATE: _____ LOCATION: _____

WHAT HAPPENED? _____
_____
_____
_____
_____

WHAT WE LOVED: _____
_____
_____
_____

WHAT WE LEARNED:_____
_____
_____

♥

53

_____
_____
_____

WHY DO WE WANT TO DO THIS? _____
_____
_____

WHAT DO WE NEED TO DO TO PREPARE?
_____
_____

♥ WE DID IT! ♥

DATE: _____ LOCATION: _____

WHAT HAPPENED? _____
_____
_____
_____
_____

WHAT WE LOVED: _____
_____
_____
_____

WHAT WE LEARNED: _____
_____
_____

♥

54

_____
_____
_____

WHY DO WE WANT TO DO THIS? _____
_____
_____

WHAT DO WE NEED TO DO TO PREPARE?
_____
_____

 ♥ WE DID IT! ♥

DATE: _____ LOCATION: _____

WHAT HAPPENED? _____
_____
_____
_____
_____

WHAT WE LOVED: _____
_____
_____
_____

WHAT WE LEARNED: _____
_____
_____
_____

♥

55

_____
_____
_____

WHY DO WE WANT TO DO THIS? _____
_____
_____

WHAT DO WE NEED TO DO TO PREPARE?
_____
_____

♥ WE DID IT! ♥

DATE: _____ LOCATION: _____

WHAT HAPPENED? _____
_____
_____
_____
_____

WHAT WE LOVED: _____
_____
_____
_____

WHAT WE LEARNED: _____
_____
_____

♥

56

_____

_____

_____

WHY DO WE WANT TO DO THIS? _____

_____

_____

WHAT DO WE NEED TO DO TO PREPARE?

_____

_____

 WE DID IT!

DATE: _____ LOCATION: _____

WHAT HAPPENED? _____

_____

_____

_____

_____

WHAT WE LOVED: _____

_____

_____

_____

WHAT WE LEARNED: _____

_____

_____

57

_____
_____
_____

WHY DO WE WANT TO DO THIS? _____
_____
_____

WHAT DO WE NEED TO DO TO PREPARE?
_____
_____

♥ WE DID IT! ♥

DATE: _____ LOCATION: _____

WHAT HAPPENED? _____
_____
_____
_____
_____

WHAT WE LOVED: _____
_____
_____
_____

WHAT WE LEARNED: _____
_____
_____

♥

58

_____
_____
_____

WHY DO WE WANT TO DO THIS? _____
_____
_____

WHAT DO WE NEED TO DO TO PREPARE?
_____
_____

♥ WE DID IT! ♥

DATE: _____ LOCATION: _____

WHAT HAPPENED? _____
_____
_____
_____

WHAT WE LOVED: _____
_____
_____

WHAT WE LEARNED: _____
_____
_____

♥

59

_____
_____
_____

WHY DO WE WANT TO DO THIS? _____

_____

_____

WHAT DO WE NEED TO DO TO PREPARE?

_____

_____

 WE DID IT! ♥

DATE: _____ LOCATION: _____

WHAT HAPPENED? _____

_____

_____

_____

_____

WHAT WE LOVED: _____

_____

_____

_____

WHAT WE LEARNED:_____

_____

_____

60

_____
_____
_____

WHY DO WE WANT TO DO THIS? _____
_____
_____

WHAT DO WE NEED TO DO TO PREPARE?
_____
_____

 **WE DID IT!**

DATE: _____ LOCATION: _____

WHAT HAPPENED? _____
_____
_____
_____
_____

WHAT WE LOVED: _____
_____
_____
_____

WHAT WE LEARNED: _____
_____
_____

68

WHY DO WE WANT TO DO THIS? _____
_____
_____

WHAT DO WE NEED TO DO TO PREPARE?
_____
_____

 WE DID IT! ♥

DATE: _____ LOCATION: _____

WHAT HAPPENED? _____
_____
_____
_____
_____

WHAT WE LOVED: _____
_____
_____
_____

WHAT WE LEARNED:_____
_____
_____

♥

67

_____
_____
_____

WHY DO WE WANT TO DO THIS? _____
_____
_____

WHAT DO WE NEED TO DO TO PREPARE?
_____
_____

 ♥ WE DID IT! ♥

DATE: _____ LOCATION: _____
WHAT HAPPENED? _____
_____
_____
_____
_____

WHAT WE LOVED: _____
_____
_____
_____

WHAT WE LEARNED:_____
_____
_____

♥

66

_____

_____

_____

WHY DO WE WANT TO DO THIS? _____

_____

_____

WHAT DO WE NEED TO DO TO PREPARE?

_____

_____

♥ WE DID IT! ♥

DATE: _____ LOCATION: _____

WHAT HAPPENED? _____

_____

_____

_____

_____

WHAT WE LOVED: _____

_____

_____

_____

WHAT WE LEARNED:_____

_____

_____

♥

65

_____

_____

_____

WHY DO WE WANT TO DO THIS? _____

_____

_____

WHAT DO WE NEED TO DO TO PREPARE?

_____

_____

♥ WE DID IT! ♥

DATE: _____ LOCATION: _____

WHAT HAPPENED? _____

_____

_____

_____

_____

WHAT WE LOVED: _____

_____

_____

_____

WHAT WE LEARNED:_____

_____

_____

♥

64

_____
_____
_____

WHY DO WE WANT TO DO THIS? _____
_____
_____

WHAT DO WE NEED TO DO TO PREPARE?
_____
_____

♥ WE DID IT! ♥

DATE: _____ LOCATION: _____

WHAT HAPPENED? _____
_____
_____
_____
_____

WHAT WE LOVED: _____
_____
_____

WHAT WE LEARNED:_____
_____
_____

63

_____

_____

_____

WHY DO WE WANT TO DO THIS? _____

_____

_____

WHAT DO WE NEED TO DO TO PREPARE?

_____

_____

 WE DID IT! ♥

DATE: _____ LOCATION: _____

WHAT HAPPENED? _____

_____

_____

_____

_____

WHAT WE LOVED: _____

_____

_____

_____

WHAT WE LEARNED:_____

_____

_____

♥

62

_____
_____
_____

WHY DO WE WANT TO DO THIS? _____
_____
_____

WHAT DO WE NEED TO DO TO PREPARE?
_____
_____

♥ WE DID IT! ♥

DATE: _____ LOCATION: _____

WHAT HAPPENED? _____
_____
_____
_____
_____

WHAT WE LOVED: _____
_____
_____
_____

WHAT WE LEARNED: _____
_____
_____

♥

61

_____
_____
_____

WHY DO WE WANT TO DO THIS? _____
_____
_____

WHAT DO WE NEED TO DO TO PREPARE?
_____
_____

♥ WE DID IT! ♥

DATE: _____ LOCATION: _____
WHAT HAPPENED? _____
_____
_____
_____
_____

WHAT WE LOVED: _____
_____
_____
_____

WHAT WE LEARNED:_____
_____
_____

♥

69

_____
_____
_____

WHY DO WE WANT TO DO THIS? _____
_____
_____

WHAT DO WE NEED TO DO TO PREPARE?
_____
_____

♥ WE DID IT! ♥

DATE: _____ LOCATION: _____

WHAT HAPPENED? _____
_____
_____
_____
_____

WHAT WE LOVED: _____
_____
_____
_____

WHAT WE LEARNED: _____
_____
_____

♥

70

_____
_____
_____
_____

WHY DO WE WANT TO DO THIS? _____
_____
_____

WHAT DO WE NEED TO DO TO PREPARE?
_____
_____

♥ WE DID IT! ♥

DATE: _____ LOCATION: _____

WHAT HAPPENED? _____
_____
_____
_____
_____

WHAT WE LOVED: _____
_____
_____
_____

WHAT WE LEARNED: _____
_____
_____

♥

71

_____
_____
_____

WHY DO WE WANT TO DO THIS? _____
_____
_____

WHAT DO WE NEED TO DO TO PREPARE?
_____
_____

 WE DID IT!

DATE: _____ LOCATION: _____

WHAT HAPPENED? _____
_____
_____
_____
_____

WHAT WE LOVED: _____
_____
_____
_____

WHAT WE LEARNED:_____
_____
_____

72

_____
_____
_____

WHY DO WE WANT TO DO THIS? _____
_____
_____

WHAT DO WE NEED TO DO TO PREPARE?
_____
_____

 WE DID IT! ♥

DATE: _____ LOCATION: _____

WHAT HAPPENED? _____
_____
_____
_____
_____

WHAT WE LOVED: _____
_____
_____
_____

WHAT WE LEARNED: _____
_____
_____

♥

73

_____
_____
_____

WHY DO WE WANT TO DO THIS? _____
_____
_____

WHAT DO WE NEED TO DO TO PREPARE?
_____
_____

♥ WE DID IT! ♥

DATE: _____ LOCATION: _____

WHAT HAPPENED? _____
_____
_____
_____
_____

WHAT WE LOVED: _____
_____
_____
_____

WHAT WE LEARNED: _____
_____
_____

♥

74

_____
_____
_____

WHY DO WE WANT TO DO THIS? _____
_____
_____

WHAT DO WE NEED TO DO TO PREPARE?
_____
_____

 WE DID IT!

DATE: _____ LOCATION: _____

WHAT HAPPENED? _____
_____
_____
_____
_____

WHAT WE LOVED: _____
_____
_____
_____

WHAT WE LEARNED: _____
_____
_____

75

_____
_____
_____

WHY DO WE WANT TO DO THIS? _____
_____
_____

WHAT DO WE NEED TO DO TO PREPARE?
_____
_____

♥ WE DID IT! ♥

DATE: _____   LOCATION: _____

WHAT HAPPENED? _____
_____
_____
_____
_____

WHAT WE LOVED: _____
_____
_____
_____

WHAT WE LEARNED:_____
_____
_____

♥

76

_____
_____
_____

WHY DO WE WANT TO DO THIS? _____
_____
_____

WHAT DO WE NEED TO DO TO PREPARE?
_____
_____

♥ WE DID IT! ♥

DATE: _____ LOCATION: _____

WHAT HAPPENED? _____
_____
_____
_____
_____

WHAT WE LOVED: _____
_____
_____
_____

WHAT WE LEARNED: _____
_____
_____

♥

77

_____
_____
_____

WHY DO WE WANT TO DO THIS? _____
_____
_____

WHAT DO WE NEED TO DO TO PREPARE?
_____
_____

 WE DID IT! 💗

DATE: _____ LOCATION: _____

WHAT HAPPENED? _____
_____
_____
_____
_____

WHAT WE LOVED: _____
_____
_____
_____

WHAT WE LEARNED:_____
_____
_____

💗

78

_____
_____
_____

WHY DO WE WANT TO DO THIS? _____
_____
_____

WHAT DO WE NEED TO DO TO PREPARE?
_____
_____

♥ WE DID IT! ♥

DATE: _____ LOCATION: _____

WHAT HAPPENED? _____
_____
_____
_____
_____

WHAT WE LOVED: _____
_____
_____

WHAT WE LEARNED: _____
_____
_____

♥

79

_____
_____
_____

WHY DO WE WANT TO DO THIS? _____
_____
_____

WHAT DO WE NEED TO DO TO PREPARE?
_____
_____

 WE DID IT! ♥

DATE: _____ LOCATION: _____
WHAT HAPPENED? _____
_____
_____
_____
_____

WHAT WE LOVED: _____
_____
_____
_____

WHAT WE LEARNED:_____
_____
_____

♥

80

_____
_____
_____

WHY DO WE WANT TO DO THIS? _____
_____
_____

WHAT DO WE NEED TO DO TO PREPARE?
_____
_____

♥ WE DID IT! ♥

DATE: _____ LOCATION: _____

WHAT HAPPENED? _____
_____
_____
_____
_____

WHAT WE LOVED: _____
_____
_____
_____

WHAT WE LEARNED:_____
_____
_____

♥

81

_____
_____
_____

WHY DO WE WANT TO DO THIS? _____
_____
_____

WHAT DO WE NEED TO DO TO PREPARE?
_____
_____

♥ WE DID IT! ♥

DATE: _____ LOCATION: _____

WHAT HAPPENED? _____
_____
_____
_____
_____

WHAT WE LOVED: _____
_____
_____
_____

WHAT WE LEARNED:_____
_____
_____

♥

82

_____
_____
_____

WHY DO WE WANT TO DO THIS? _____
_____
_____

WHAT DO WE NEED TO DO TO PREPARE?
_____
_____

♥ WE DID IT! ♥

DATE: _____ LOCATION: _____

WHAT HAPPENED? _____
_____
_____
_____
_____

WHAT WE LOVED: _____
_____
_____
_____

WHAT WE LEARNED:_____
_____
_____

♥

83

_____
_____
_____

WHY DO WE WANT TO DO THIS? _____
_____
_____

WHAT DO WE NEED TO DO TO PREPARE?
_____
_____

 ♥ WE DID IT! ♥

DATE: _____ LOCATION: _____
WHAT HAPPENED? _____
_____
_____
_____
_____

WHAT WE LOVED: _____
_____
_____
_____

WHAT WE LEARNED: _____
_____
_____

♥

84

_____
_____
_____

WHY DO WE WANT TO DO THIS? _____
_____
_____

WHAT DO WE NEED TO DO TO PREPARE?
_____
_____

♥ WE DID IT! ♥

DATE: _____ LOCATION: _____

WHAT HAPPENED? _____
_____
_____
_____
_____

WHAT WE LOVED: _____
_____
_____

WHAT WE LEARNED: _____
_____
_____

♥

85

_____
_____
_____

WHY DO WE WANT TO DO THIS? _____
_____
_____

WHAT DO WE NEED TO DO TO PREPARE?
_____
_____

 WE DID IT! ♥

DATE: _____ LOCATION: _____

WHAT HAPPENED? _____
_____
_____
_____
_____

WHAT WE LOVED: _____
_____
_____
_____

WHAT WE LEARNED: _____
_____
_____

♥

86 _____
_____
_____

WHY DO WE WANT TO DO THIS? _____
_____
_____

WHAT DO WE NEED TO DO TO PREPARE?
_____
_____

♥ WE DID IT! ♥

DATE: _____   LOCATION: _____

WHAT HAPPENED? _____
_____
_____
_____
_____

WHAT WE LOVED: _____
_____
_____
_____

WHAT WE LEARNED:_____
_____
_____

♥

87

_____
_____
_____

WHY DO WE WANT TO DO THIS? _____

_____

_____

WHAT DO WE NEED TO DO TO PREPARE?

_____

_____

 WE DID IT! 🩶

DATE: _____   LOCATION: _____

WHAT HAPPENED? _____

_____

_____

_____

_____

WHAT WE LOVED: _____

_____

_____

_____

WHAT WE LEARNED:_____

_____

_____

🩶

88

_____
_____
_____

WHY DO WE WANT TO DO THIS? _____
_____
_____

WHAT DO WE NEED TO DO TO PREPARE?
_____
_____

♥ WE DID IT! ♥

DATE: _____ LOCATION: _____

WHAT HAPPENED? _____
_____
_____
_____
_____

WHAT WE LOVED: _____
_____
_____
_____

WHAT WE LEARNED:_____
_____
_____

♥

89 _____
_____
_____

WHY DO WE WANT TO DO THIS? _____
_____
_____

WHAT DO WE NEED TO DO TO PREPARE?
_____
_____

♥ WE DID IT! ♥

DATE: _____ LOCATION: _____
WHAT HAPPENED? _____
_____
_____
_____
_____

WHAT WE LOVED: _____
_____
_____
_____

WHAT WE LEARNED:_____
_____
_____

♥

90

_____
_____
_____

WHY DO WE WANT TO DO THIS? _____
_____
_____

WHAT DO WE NEED TO DO TO PREPARE?
_____
_____

♥ WE DID IT! ♥

DATE: _____ LOCATION: _____

WHAT HAPPENED? _____
_____
_____
_____
_____

WHAT WE LOVED: _____
_____
_____
_____

WHAT WE LEARNED: _____
_____
_____

♥

91

_____
_____
_____

WHY DO WE WANT TO DO THIS? _____
_____
_____

WHAT DO WE NEED TO DO TO PREPARE?
_____
_____

 ♥ **WE DID IT!** ♥

DATE: _____ LOCATION: _____
WHAT HAPPENED? _____
_____
_____
_____
_____

WHAT WE LOVED: _____
_____
_____

WHAT WE LEARNED: _____
_____
_____

♥

92

_____
_____
_____

WHY DO WE WANT TO DO THIS? _____
_____
_____

WHAT DO WE NEED TO DO TO PREPARE?
_____
_____

♥ WE DID IT! ♥

DATE: _____ LOCATION: _____
WHAT HAPPENED? _____
_____
_____
_____
_____

WHAT WE LOVED: _____
_____
_____

WHAT WE LEARNED:_____
_____
_____

♥

93

_____
_____
_____

WHY DO WE WANT TO DO THIS? _____
_____
_____

WHAT DO WE NEED TO DO TO PREPARE?
_____
_____

♥ WE DID IT! ♥

DATE: _____ LOCATION: _____

WHAT HAPPENED? _____
_____
_____
_____
_____

WHAT WE LOVED: _____
_____
_____
_____

WHAT WE LEARNED: _____
_____
_____

♥

94

_____

_____

_____

WHY DO WE WANT TO DO THIS? _____

_____

_____

WHAT DO WE NEED TO DO TO PREPARE?

_____

_____

♥ WE DID IT! ♥

DATE: _____ LOCATION: _____

WHAT HAPPENED? _____

_____

_____

_____

_____

WHAT WE LOVED: _____

_____

_____

WHAT WE LEARNED: _____

_____

_____

♥

95

_____
_____
_____

WHY DO WE WANT TO DO THIS? _____
_____
_____

WHAT DO WE NEED TO DO TO PREPARE?
_____
_____

♥ WE DID IT! ♥

DATE: _____ LOCATION: _____

WHAT HAPPENED? _____
_____
_____
_____
_____

WHAT WE LOVED: _____
_____
_____
_____

WHAT WE LEARNED:_____
_____
_____

♥

96

_____
_____
_____

WHY DO WE WANT TO DO THIS? _____
_____
_____

WHAT DO WE NEED TO DO TO PREPARE?
_____
_____

♥ WE DID IT! ♥

DATE: _____ LOCATION: _____

WHAT HAPPENED? _____
_____
_____
_____
_____

WHAT WE LOVED: _____
_____
_____
_____

WHAT WE LEARNED: _____
_____
_____

♥

97

_____
_____
_____
_____

WHY DO WE WANT TO DO THIS? _____
_____
_____

WHAT DO WE NEED TO DO TO PREPARE?
_____
_____

 WE DID IT! ♥

DATE: _____ LOCATION: _____

WHAT HAPPENED? _____
_____
_____
_____
_____

WHAT WE LOVED: _____
_____
_____
_____

WHAT WE LEARNED:_____
_____
_____
_____

♥

98

_____
_____
_____

WHY DO WE WANT TO DO THIS? _____
_____
_____

WHAT DO WE NEED TO DO TO PREPARE?
_____
_____

 WE DID IT!

DATE: _____ LOCATION: _____
WHAT HAPPENED? _____
_____
_____
_____
_____

WHAT WE LOVED: _____
_____
_____

WHAT WE LEARNED:_____
_____
_____

99

_____
_____
_____
_____

WHY DO WE WANT TO DO THIS? _____
_____
_____

WHAT DO WE NEED TO DO TO PREPARE?
_____
_____

♥ WE DID IT! ♥

DATE: _____ LOCATION: _____

WHAT HAPPENED? _____
_____
_____
_____
_____

WHAT WE LOVED: _____
_____
_____
_____

WHAT WE LEARNED: _____
_____
_____

♥

100 _____
_____
_____

WHY DO WE WANT TO DO THIS? _____
_____
_____

WHAT DO WE NEED TO DO TO PREPARE?
_____
_____

♥ WE DID IT! ♥

DATE: _____ LOCATION: _____

WHAT HAPPENED? _____
_____
_____
_____
_____

WHAT WE LOVED: _____
_____
_____
_____

WHAT WE LEARNED:_____
_____
_____

♥

Other
Notes